The
United Nations

Global Leadership

Humanitarian Relief Operations

Lending a Helping Hand

by Roger Smith

Mason Crest Publishers
Philadelphia

Mason Crest Publishers Inc.
370 Reed Road
Broomall, Pennsylvania 19008
(866) MCP-BOOK (toll free)

First printing
1 2 3 4 5 6 7 8 9 10

Library of Congress Cataloging-in-Publication Data

Smith, Roger, 1959 Aug. 15–
    Humanitarian relief operations : lending a helping hand / by Roger Smith.
        p. cm. — (United Nations—global leadership)
    Includes bibliographical references and index.
    ISBN 1-4222-0070-1 ISBN 1-4222-0065-5 (series)
    1. Humanitarian assistance. 2. Humanitarian intervention. 3. International relief. 4. United Nations. Dept. of Humanitarian Affairs. I. Title. II. Series.
    HV553.S58 2007
    361.6—dc22
                                    2006001308

Interior design by Benjamin Stewart.
Interiors produced by Harding House Publishing Service, Inc.
www.hardinghousepages.com
Cover design by Peter Culatta.
Printed in the Hashemite Kingdom of Jordan.

Contents

Introduction
by Dr. Bruce Russett

The United Nations was founded in 1945 by the victors of World War II. They hoped the new organization could learn from the mistakes of the League of Nations that followed World War I—and prevent another war.

The United Nations has not been able to bring worldwide peace; that would be an unrealistic hope. But it has contributed in important ways to the world's experience of more than sixty years without a new world war. Despite its flaws, the United Nations has contributed to peace.

Like any big organization, the United Nations is composed of many separate units with different jobs. These units make three different kinds of contributions. The most obvious to students in North America and other democracies are those that can have a direct and immediate impact for peace.

Especially prominent is the Security Council, which is the only UN unit that can authorize the use of military force against countries and can require all UN members to cooperate in isolating an aggressor country's economy. In the Security Council, each of the big powers—Britain, China, France, Russia, and the United States—can veto any proposed action. That's because the founders of United Nations recognized that if the Council tried to take any military action against the strong opposition of a big power it would result in war. As a result, the United Nations was often sidelined during the Cold War era. Since the end of the Cold War in 1990, however, the Council has authorized many military actions, some directed against specific aggressors but most intended as more neutral peacekeeping efforts. Most of its peacekeeping efforts have been to end civil wars rather than wars between countries. Not all have succeeded, but many have. The United Nations Secretary-General also has had an important role in mediating some conflicts.

UN units that promote trade and economic development make a different kind of contribution. Some help to establish free markets for greater prosperity, or like the UN Development Programme, provide economic and technical assistance to reduce poverty in poor countries. Some are especially concerned with environmental problems or health issues. For example, the World Health Organization and UNICEF deserve great credit for eliminating the deadly disease of smallpox from the world. Poor countries especially support the United Nations for this reason. Since many wars, within and between countries, stem from economic deprivation, these efforts make an important indirect contribution to peace.

Still other units make a third contribution: they promote human rights. The High Commission for Refugees, for example, has worked to ease the distress of millions of refugees who have fled their countries to escape from war and political persecution. A special unit of the Secretary-General's office has supervised and assisted free elections in more than ninety countries. It tries to establish stable and democratic governments in newly independent countries or in countries where the people have defeated a dictatorial government. Other units promote the rights of women, children, and religious and ethnic minorities. The General Assembly provides a useful setting for debate on these and other issues.

These three kinds of action—to end violence, to reduce poverty, and to promote social and political justice—all make a contribution to peace. True peace requires all three, working together.

The UN does not always succeed: like individuals, it makes mistakes . . . and it often learns from its mistakes. Despite the United Nations' occasional stumbles, over the years it has grown and moved forward. These books will show you how.

The 2004 tsunami left terrible destruction in its wake.

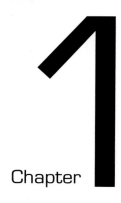

Chapter 1

The UN Charter and the UN's Role in Humanitarian Relief

The Asian tsunami of December 26, 2004, was one of the worst natural disasters in modern history. An underground earthquake began tidal waves that killed more than 200,000 people in countries of Indonesia, Sri Lanka, India, Thailand, Somalia, the Maldives, Myanmar, and the Seychelles Islands.

A house in Banda Aceh, Indonesia, that was destroyed by the tsunami

Chapter One—The UN Charter and the UN's Role in Humanitarian Relief

Hafun, a fishing village in northeast Somalia, was one place hit by the tsunami. One resident of Hafun, nine-year-old Faduma Farah Aden, wanted to go to school but never believed she would have a chance to do so; most of the girls in Hafun have to spend their days looking after sheep and fetching firewood. UNICEF worker Alhaji Bah reports on the UNICEF Somalia site, "Following the disaster of 26 December 2004, UNICEF supported the establishment of temporary classrooms in Hafun. . . . After their lives were disrupted by the tsunami, the girls were encouraged to attend school. . . . Faduma jumped at the opportunity."

For sixty years, the United Nations has worked through its various agencies to bring relief and assistance where people are hungry, lack shelter, education, or medical care.

UN Overview

On October 24, 1945, fifty-one countries committed to preserving peace through international cooperation established the United Nations. By 2005, almost every nation in the world belonged to the organization, and its membership totalled 191 countries.

When countries join the United Nations, they agree to follow the UN Charter. The Charter says that the United Nations has four purposes: to maintain international peace and security; to develop friendly relations among nations; to cooperate in solving international problems and in promoting respect for human rights; and to be a center for harmonizing the actions of nations.

The United Nations does not make laws and it is not a world government; however, it does provide ways to help nations resolve conflicts between them. All the UN members—large and small, rich and poor, with a variety of political views and social systems—participate and vote in this process.

The United Nations has six main parts. Five of them are based at the UN Headquarters in New York City: these are the General Assembly, the Security Council, the Economic and Social Council, the Trusteeship Council, and the Secretariat. The International Court of Justice is located at The Hague in the Netherlands.

The General Assembly, which represents all member nations, is a "parliament of nations" that meets to consider the world's most pressing problems. Each member nation holds one vote. Together, they make decisions on vital issues such as international peace and security by two-thirds majority; they decide other matters by simple majority.

The Security Council of the United Nations holds the major responsibility for maintaining international peace. The council may get together whenever peace is threatened. The UN Charter obligates all member nations to carry out decisions made by the council. Of the fifteen members

Millennium Development Goals and Targets (MDGs)

- **Eradicate extreme poverty and hunger:** By 2015, reduce by half the proportion of people living on less than $1 a day and the share suffering from hunger.
- **Achieve universal primary education:** Ensure that by 2015 all boys and girls complete a full course of primary schooling.
- **Promote gender equality and empower women:** Eliminate gender disparity in primary and secondary education, preferably by 2005, and at all levels by 2015.
- **Reduce child mortality**. By 2015, reduce by two-thirds the mortality rate among children under five.
- **Improve maternal health:** By 2015, reduce by three-quarters the maternal mortality rate.
- **Combat HIV/AIDS, malaria and other diseases.** Halt and begin to reverse the spread of HIV/AIDS, malaria and other major diseases by 2015.
- **Ensure environmental sustainability**. Integrate the principles of sustainable development into country policies and programs and reverse the loss of environmental resources. By 2015, cut in half the proportion of people without sustainable access to safe drinking water and sanitation. By 2020, improve significantly the lives of 100 million slum dwellers.
- **Develop a global partnership for development.** Develop an open trading and financial system that is rule-based, nondiscriminatory, and includes a commitment to good governance, development, and poverty reduction.

Source: State of the World 2005, by the Worldwatch Institute.

of the Security Council, five—China, France, the Russian Federation, the United Kingdom, and the United States—are permanent members, and members elect the other ten. The permanent members of the Security Council have veto power; a veto by any one of those countries defeats any proposal put before the council. When the council deals with a threat to peace, it begins by exploring ways to settle the problem peacefully, such as working to mediate (make peace) between parties in a conflict. If parties are fighting, the council tries to make them agree to a cease-fire. In very bad situations, the council may send a peacekeeping mission to maintain a cease-fire between par-

One of the Millennium Development goals is that all children, no matter where they live, will be able to complete primary school.

*Aspects of the Economic and Social Council of the United Nations'
focus on environmental issues.*

The United Nations works for the protection of women's rights around the world.

ties or to keep opposing forces apart. The council can also impose economic sanctions (forbidding other nations to trade with a nation) or order an arms embargo (forbidding other nations to sell weapons to a country).

The General Assembly elects fifty-four members for three-year terms on the Economic and Social Council, which directs the economic and social work of UN organizations. This council is the most important means for discussing international economic and social issues; it plays a vital role in promoting international cooperation for development. It also works with ***nongovernmental organizations (NGOs)***. The council meets throughout the year, and other branches of the UN report to it regularly. For example, the Commission on Human Rights reports violations of human rights around the world. Other bodies focus on such issues as social development, the status of women, crime prevention, narcotic drugs, and environmental protection.

A UN civil education team travels by boat to a remote island.

Chapter One—The UN Charter and the UN's Role in Humanitarian Relief

The UN Charter and Humanitarian Relief

In its preamble (opening words), it is written that the UN Charter is an agreement not among "governments" or "countries" but between "the peoples" of the world. It emphasizes the need for peace, human rights, and better living standards around the globe, saying the United Nations will "reaffirm faith in fundamental human rights, in the dignity and worth of the human person, in the equal rights of men and women and of nations large and small." Article 1 of the charter includes among the purposes of the United Nations, "To achieve international co-operation in solving international problems of an economic, social, cultural, or *humanitarian* character, and in promoting and encouraging respect for human rights and for fundamental freedoms for all without distinction as to race, sex, language, or religion."

Millennium Assembly Goals for Improving World Health and Social Development

A special gathering of the UN General Assembly took place in September of 2000; this was the Millennium Assembly, gathered to set goals to reduce global poverty, disease, and unfair treatment of people by the year 2015. It came up with a document titled Millennium Development Goals and Targets.

According to a report by Hilary French, Gary Gardner, and Erik Assadourian in the Worldwatch Institute's *State of the World 2005*, "While the commitment on paper to achieving the MGDs is strong, progress for the most part has been excruciatingly slow." So far, the world has not put in all of the effort necessary to achieve these goals. Less than one-fifth of all countries are on schedule to reduce child and maternal mortality or provide access to water and sanitation by their target dates. The goals for reducing HIV/AIDS, malaria, and other major diseases are even further behind.

UN Agencies and Humanitarian Relief

When disasters strike, UN organizations and NGOs that work with them supply food, shelter, medicines, and practical support to the victims, many of whom are children, women, and the elderly. To pay for this help, the United Nations raises billions of dollars from donors around the world. In 2001, the Office for the Coordination of Humanitarian Affairs sent out nineteen appeals for money to help relief efforts. They succeeded in raising more than $1.4 billion to assist 44 million people in nineteen different nations.

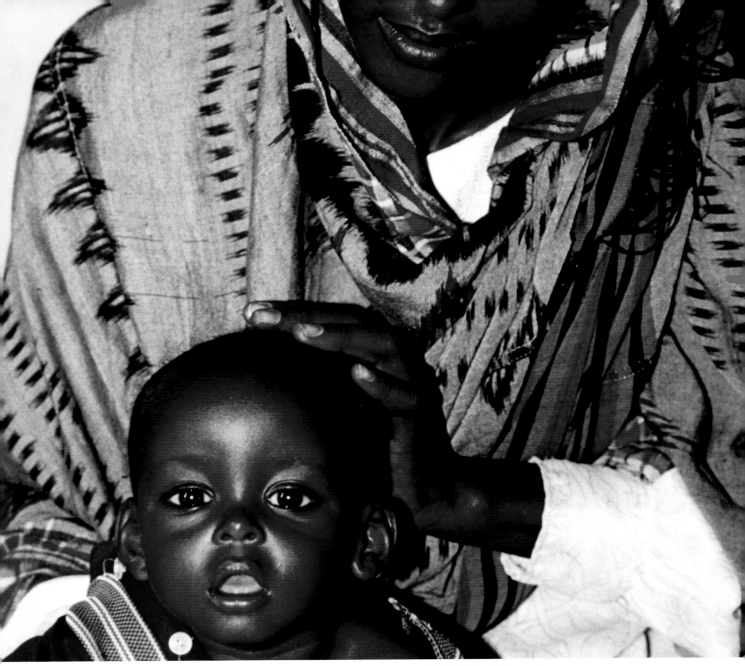
A mother and child await food at a UNICEF relief center.

Wars and human rights abuses often make it difficult to deliver humanitarian aid. Soldiers and *guerrillas* sometimes target relief workers who are trying to deliver food or medicine to people in need. Since 1992, more than 200 UN relief workers have been killed and some 265 taken hostage while attempting to deliver aid to people in need around the world. Trying to protect aid workers in dangerous places, the UN High Commissioner for Human Rights (UNHCHR) has played an increasingly active role in the UN response to emergencies. The UNHCHR stands up for human rights and coordinates UN programs dealing with human rights.

The UN Centre for Human Rights is one of the most important offices under the UNHCHR. The Centre is located in Geneva, Switzerland, and provides suggestions and information for all the other programs, offices, and agencies under the UNHCHR.

The United Nations responds to disasters and humanitarian crises through a committee that includes all of its vital relief and development groups, chaired by the UN Emergency Relief Coordinator. These various groups include the UN Children's Fund (UNICEF), the UN Development Programme (UNDP), the UN Relief and Works Agency for Palestine Refugees in the Near East (NRWA), the World Food Programme (WFP), and the UN High Commissioner for Refugees (UNHCR).

The UNHCR assists refugees and *displaced persons*, people who have fled war, persecution, or human rights abuse. According to the UN.org Web site, "At the start of 2001, there were some 22 million people of concern to UNHCR in more than 120 countries, including some 5.4 million *internally displaced.* Some 3.6 million Afghans accounted for 30 percent of refugees worldwide, followed by 568,000 refugees from Burundi and 512,800 from Iraq."

The World Food Programme (WFP) is the world's largest food aid organization, supplying one-third of emergency food assistance worldwide. In 2000, it delivered 3.7 million tons of food to 83 million people in eighty-three different nations.

UNICEF seeks to meet the needs of an estimated 1 million children separated from their parents by war and large-scale violence over the past decade. It aids these children by supplying food, safe water, medicine, and shelter.

A UN resettlement camp in Natal

Chapter 2

Humanitarian Assistance Programs

Threshold The UNDP Web site in 2005 gave this story from Afghanistan:

Water drips in a slow tip-tap into a red bucket standing on the white marble of a brand new public bathhouse in the northern city of Mazar-i-Sharif, in Afghanistan. Forty-year-old Mohammed Sarder, gently shampooing his four-year-old son, Azar, smiles and says "it's my first bath in six years." Public bathhouses or hammams have served for hundreds of years as community hygiene centres and public forums. . . . Public bathing was considered a crime under the Taliban regime; therefore, communities were denied this important hygiene and social forum. . . . In 2003, the United Nations Development Programme (UNDP) initiated a project—with funds from the European Commission—to construct and rehabilitate 19 hammams in the major cities of Mazar-i-Sharif in the north, Kandahar in the south and Jalalabad in the east. . . . Hammams are experiencing a major rebirth as thousands of men and women in Afghanistan, who lack access to hot, clean, running water, return en masse to this traditional form of bathing.

UN support helps build a new home in Ethiopia.

What do actors Danny Glover, Angelina Jolie, and Jackie Chan have in common with former Spice Girl Geri Halliwell and former boxer Muhammed Ali? They have all been UN Goodwill Ambassadors. Ever since the late actor/singer Danny Kaye was named the first Goodwill Ambassador in 1954, celebrities from entertainment, sports, and the arts have volunteered their time to promote UN programs.

The UNDP was founded in 1945 and is based in New York City. The UNDP focuses on four aspects of development: poverty, environment, jobs, and women. In 2005, the UNDP worked in 166 different countries, and it was involved in every African nation. In Burkina Faso, it provided villages with a diesel-fueled machine that helps village women perform hard jobs such as grinding grains and collecting water. The government of Burkina Faso, in collaboration with the UNDP, started 400 businesses that use these platforms. These businesses are mostly founded and run by women, employ 4,000 people and benefit around 500,000 villagers across the country. In Somalia, the UNDP cooperated with the government to open the first new police academy in that nation in recent years. "This is a momentous occasion for us," Prime Minister Ali Mohamed Gedi said. He continued:

> The young women and men who will come out of this training will form part of the new Somalia, where the rights of every Somali are protected and the rule of law will prevail. We cannot waiver in our quest to change the way things have been for the last decade and a half and more.

The UNDP also has offices in twenty-four countries in Latin America and the Caribbean, where it supports forty-four different programs. In 2005, a donation from soccer stars Ronaldo and Zidane, both of them UNDP Goodwill Ambassadors, provided school materials and supplies to children living in the most populated slum area in Haiti. The UNDP also works in thirty-three countries in Asia and Pacific regions.

Who Is a Refugee?

A refugee is a person who "owing to a well-founded fear of being persecuted for reasons of race, religion, nationality, membership of a particular social group, or political opinion, is outside the country of his nationality, and is unable to or, owing to such fear, is unwilling to avail himself of the protection of that country."
—*The 1951 Convention relating to the Status of Refugees*

UNHCR

According to the UNHCR Web site:

> Every country in the world has been affected by a refugee crisis. States directly involved in war produced millions of uprooted peoples in the last century alone. Other countries, untouched by chaos themselves, provided aid and shelter to the displaced. The roles have sometimes been reversed. Europe was awash with refugees in the aftermath of two world wars, but later became a beacon of hope to other ***disenfranchised*** people.
>
> In many cases, today's neighbor is tomorrow's refugee. They have lost their homes, jobs, community and often family. They are not a threat, but they do need temporary help until they can re-establish their lives. The great majority of people wish to return to their own homes once the situation there normalizes. But if a refugee does stay for whatever reason, he or she can often become a valuable asset to a community. A Who's Who of the world's leading businessmen, artists and politicians includes many former refugees.

The word refugee refers specifically to people who have fled their homeland and sought refuge in a second country. However, there are also an estimated 20 to 25 million so-called internally displaced persons (IDPs) around the globe, people who have fled their homes during a civil war, but have stayed in their native countries rather than seek refuge abroad.

According to the UNHCR Web site:

> At the start of the year 2005, the number of people of concern to UNHCR was 19.2 million. They included 9.2 million refugees (48%), 839,200 asylum seekers (4%), 1.5 million returned refugees (8%), 5.6 million internally displaced persons (29%) and 2 million others of concern (11%).

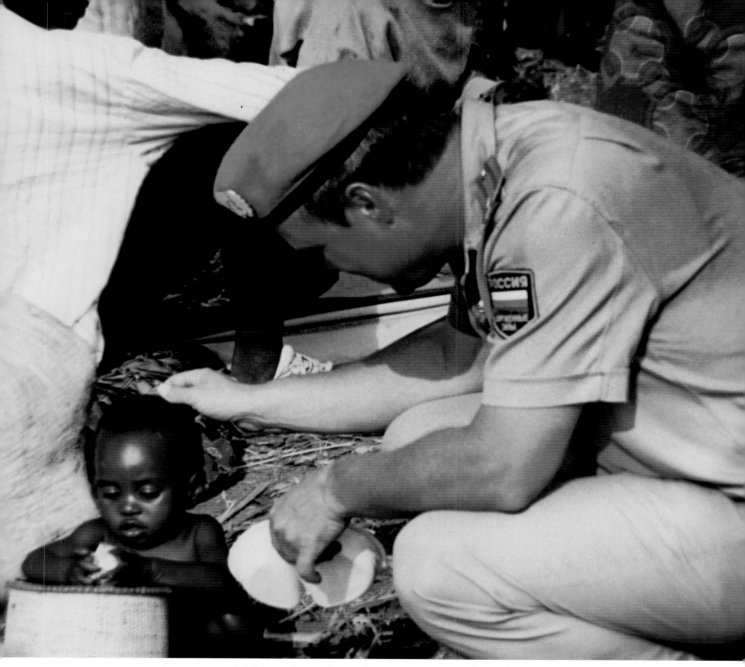

A UN worker at a refugee camp in Rwanda

A refugee boy in Damascus after World War II

On December 14, 1950, the UN General Assembly established the Office of the United Nations High Commissioner for Refugees. The agency leads international action to protect refugees and resolve refugee problems. In the past five decades, the agency has helped an estimated 50 million people restart their lives. In 2005, the UNHCR staff of 6,540 people in 116 countries served more than 19 million persons.

When the UNHCR was established, the new agency was given a three-year mandate to help resettle 1.2 million European refugees left homeless by World War II. However, as refugee crises continued around the globe, its mandate was extended every five years. Finally, in December 2003, the General Assembly decided to remove the time limitation on the UNHCR, since worldwide refugee situations show no sign of disappearing in the near future.

Korean refugees during the Korean War in the 1950s

Humanitarian Relief Operations: Lending a Helping Hand

In the years since the UNHCR began, the problems of displaced people became tougher and more global, so the UNHCR adapted to changing circumstances. It grew from a relatively small, specialized agency to an organization with offices in 116 countries, an annual budget of around $1 billion a year, and the ability to provide not only legal protection but also material relief for major emergencies.

The UNHCR can only offer effective legal protection to refugees if a person's basic needs such as shelter, food, water, *sanitation*, and medical care are met first. UNHCR therefore provides such items, especially for vulnerable women, children, and the elderly who make up 80 percent of most refugee populations. Tents made from UNHCR blue plastic sheeting have been seen in major emergencies in the last decade, including operations in Chad, Iraq, Afghanistan, West Africa, Timor, Kosovo, Africa's Great Lakes region, the Balkans, and in the aftermath of the Gulf War. In Central America, the UNHCR developed the idea of quick impact projects or QIPs. These projects are small-scale programs designed to bridge the gaps between emergency assistance.

The UNHCR also works to reunite unaccompanied minors with their parents. An unaccompanied minor is a child "who is separated from both parents and for whose care no person can be found who by law or custom has primary responsibility." Unaccompanied children often make up 2 to 5 percent of a refugee population. The UNHCR works with other agencies, including the Red Cross, UNICEF, and Save the Children, to help identify unaccompanied minors and reunite them with their families. In the Rwandan crisis in the mid-1990s, for instance, an estimated 67,000 children were brought back to their parents and other relatives.

The UNHCR is active throughout the world caring for a diverse range of situations. Refugees from Afghanistan, for example, were one concern of the UNHCR in 2005. Since the Taliban regime fell in 2001, more than 3.5 million Afghan refugees and displaced persons have returned home, but at least 2 million *exiles* remain in Pakistan and Iran; they are the largest single group in the world "of concern" to the UNHCR. Some 500,000 Sri Lankan refugees in India are another sizable group of concern. Disruptions and wars throughout the continent of Africa have caused millions of people in African nations to face refugee and IDP crises during the twenty-first century. The UNHCR Web site also reports that in Colombia in 2005:

> The worst humanitarian crisis in the Western Hemisphere continued to deteriorate, despite negotiations between the government and the *paramilitaries*. A peace process with the largest rebel group had not resumed since its collapse in 2002. More than 2 million people are uprooted within Colombia, while tens of thousands have sought *asylum* abroad.

A Turkish Cypriot refugee camp in Cyprus in 1964

Tomb Raider Serves with Refugees

Today, Angelina Jolie is an official Goodwill Ambassador working with UNHCR. Jolie is the star of *Mr. and Mrs. Smith*, *Tomb Raider*, and numerous other popular films. Her work with UNHCR began in 2001 with a mission to Sierra Leone, a small West African country devastated by years of civil war. Seeing firsthand the enormous challenges that refugees face altered Jolie's life, leading her to use her fame to aid their cause. Since she was named a Goodwill Ambassador later the same year, she has visited UNHCR refugee operations in the Balkans, Namibia, Tanzania, Kenya, Cambodia, Thailand, Pakistan, and Ecuador. During one of her visits, Angelina Jolie wrote, "You go to these places and you realize what life's really about and what people are really going through. These people are my heroes."

UNRWA

According to the official Web site of the UNRWA:

> UNRWA (the United Nations Relief and Works Agency for Palestine Refugees in the Near East) is a relief and human development agency, providing education, healthcare, social services and emergency aid to over four million refugees living in the Gaza Strip, the West Bank, Jordan, Lebanon and the Syrian Arab republic. UNRWA is by far the largest UN operation in the Middle East, with over 25,000 staff, almost all of them refugees themselves, working directly to benefit their communities-as teachers, doctors, nurses or social workers.

The 1948 Arab-Israeli conflict left 750,000 Palestinians without homes. Immediately after the conflict, the UN General Assembly established UNRWA to carry out direct relief and works programs for Palestinian refugees. Since the Palestinian issue has not been resolved since then, the General Assembly has repeatedly renewed UNRWA's mandate, extending it until June 2008. UNRWA differs from other UN relief and assistance agencies due to its long-standing commitment to one specific group of refugees over four generations. Currently, UNRWA is the main provider of basic services such as education, health, relief, and social services for over 4 million Palestinian refugees in the Middle East. Around a third of these refugees, some 1.3 million, live in fifty-nine camps; UNRWA's services are located in or near these camps.

Israeli troops withdrawing from Palestinian land in accordance with a UN agreement

An Israeli army jeep by the wall that divides Israel from Palestine

Unlike other UN groups that work through local authorities or executing agencies, UNRWA provides its services directly to their Palestinian refugee clients; therefore, it runs its own projects, including the building of facilities such as schools and clinics. The agency's more than 24,000 staff workers currently manage over 900 facilities.

Education accounts for more than half of UNRWA's activity and two-thirds of its staff. In the 2002–2003 school year, UNRWA provided free education to more than 490,000 young Palestinian refugees in 656 schools; more than half the students were female.

UNRWA also provides primary health care for Palestinian refugees through a network of 122 medical facilities that handled more than 9 million patient visits in 2002. Additionally, UNRWA provides environmental health services for the 1.3 million refugee camp residents; these services include sewage disposal, management of storm water runoff, provision of safe drinking water, collection and disposal of refuse, and control of insects and rodents.

Palestinian refugee families unable to meet their own basic needs also receive relief and assis-

The wall that separates Israel and Palestine actually passes through this house. Windows and doors to the Israel side are sealed. And people live in the house.

Humanitarian Relief Operations: Lending a Helping Hand

A minefield warning sign, written in Hebrew, Arabic, and English, in the Israeli desert testifies to the violence that mars this land.

tance from UNRWA. More than 233,000 persons (more than 5 percent of all Palestine refugees registered with the agency) receive assistance of this sort from UNRWA.

UNRWA also carries out special projects to improve the lives of Palestinian refugees. Two of these are the Neirab Rehabilitation project in Syria and new housing project in Tel Es-Sultan in Rafah, south Gaza. UNRWA and the European Union worked together to build the European Gaza Hospital. The 232-bed hospital near the city of Khan Younis in the Gaza Strip was completed in 1996, and new outpatient facilities were opened in July 2000. The European Union and its members contributed the funds to build this hospital.

The conflict between Israel and the Palestinian people is long, complicated, and bitter. Therefore, any agency caring for Palestinian refugees is bound to generate ***controversy***. Critics have alleged that UNRWA supports terrorists living within the refugee camps. In response, UNRWA states:

UNRWA does not run refugee camps. It is a UN agency with a clearly defined mandate, in accordance with which, it provides health, education and other humanitarian services to

Religion plays a major role in the hostilities between the Israelis and the Palestinians.

The Kuwait Towers, a national landmark, were destroyed during the Iraqi invasion, but they have since been restored.

refugees, only one third of whom live in refugee camps. . . . The Agency has no police force, no *intelligence service* and no mandate to report on political and military activities.

Policing the camps is the responsibility of either the Palestinian Authority or Israeli police, depending on the location of the specific refugee camp.

Office of the Iraq Programme

In August 1990, the Security Council imposed sanctions on Iraq following that country's invasion of Kuwait. After the Gulf War ended in 1991, the UN secretary-general, Kofi Annan, sent a group to look at humanitarian needs in Iraq and Kuwait. That group reported, "The Iraqi people may soon face a further imminent catastrophe, which could include epidemic and famine, if massive life-supporting needs are not rapidly met." In response, the Security Council set up an "oil-for-food" program, providing Iraq an opportunity to sell oil to finance the purchase of humanitarian goods. That program, started in December 1996, allowed Iraq to sell $2 billion worth of oil every six months, with two-thirds of that amount to be used to meet Iraq's humanitarian needs.

In March 2003, the Secretary-General Annan announced he could no longer guarantee the safety of UN personnel in Iraq, so they were evacuated. As the Oil-for-Food Programme ended in 2003, according to the Iraq Programme official Web site:

> "United Nations Secretary-General Kofi Annan has praised the Oil-for-Food Programme for accomplishing one of the largest, most complex and unusual tasks ever entrusted to the Secretariat. . . . He said that in nearly seven years of operation, the Programme had been required to meet "an almost impossible series of challenges," using some $46 billion of Iraqi export earnings on behalf of the Iraqi people."

Despite Annan's cheerful report on the program, numerous critics have claimed the program was largely run in a corrupt manner. A 2005 article by Nile Gardiner for the Heritage Foundation reported:

> The 55 audits produced by the Internal Audit Division (IAD) of the U.N. Office of Internal Oversight Services (OIOS) paint an ugly tableau of widespread mismanagement and incompetence on the ground in Iraq, which undoubtedly played an important role in allowing Saddam Hussein to skim billions of dollars from a humanitarian program designed to help

the Iraqi people. . . . In addition, the UN wasted millions of dollars as a result of overpayments to contractors, appalling lack of oversight, and unjustified spending.

The World Food Program (WFP)

There are more than 800 million hungry people in the world—more than all the people living in the United States and all the nations of the European Union combined. The hungry are people of all ages, from babies whose mothers cannot produce enough milk to elderly people with no relatives to care for them. They may live in urban slums or on farms that cannot produce enough food; they may be the orphans of AIDS victims.

According to the WFP's mission statement:

As the food aid arm of the UN, WFP uses its food to:

- meet emergency needs
- support economic and social development

The Agency also provides the logistics support necessary to get food aid to the right people at the right time and in the right place. WFP works to put hunger at the centre of the international agenda, promoting policies, strategies and operations that directly benefit the poor and hungry.

The WFP assists victims of natural disasters like the tsunami in 2004. It also helps displaced peoples, both refugees and internally displaced persons, who are forced to leave their own towns and villages in places like Darfur, the Democratic Republic of Congo, and Colombia. It also serves, as its Web site says, "the world's hungry poor, trapped in a twilight zone between poverty and malnutrition."

NGOs

NGOs are independent, nonprofit, voluntary associations that focus on areas of interest to the United Nations, such as human rights or relief work. In the United States they are more commonly known as "nonprofit organizations." The United Nations has become increasingly inter-

The beautiful and ancient land of Congo is torn by hunger and violence.

A relief doctor examines a baby under a mango tree in Mzizima.

ested in working with NGOs because they directly represent the citizens of the world's nations. There are nearly 2,200 NGOs that have "consultative status"; this gives them the right to participate in some UN meetings, studies, and projects. These NGOs do not become actual parts of the UN organization; most NGOs would not wish to do so because they value their ability to function independently of the United Nations.

A Few NGOs Concerned with Humanitarian Relief

CARE International is one of the world's largest relief and development organizations, operating in more than seventy countries and benefiting over 45 million people. CARE has thousands of programs around the world dealing with a variety of issues that keep people trapped in poverty, from HIV/AIDS, *discrimination*, and a lack of clean water to not being able to get a decent job. CARE has more than12,000 employees worldwide, yet more than 90 percent of CARE staff are citizens of the countries where local programs are run. CARE has no political or religious affiliation.

Médecins Sans Frontières (MSF; Doctors Without Borders) is an international humanitarian aid organization that provides emergency medical assistance to at-risk populations in more than seventy countries. Where health structures are insufficient—or nonexistent—MSF collaborates with authorities such as the Ministry of Health to provide assistance. MSF works in rehabilitation of hospitals and *dispensaries*, vaccination programs, and water and sanitation projects. MSF also trains personnel in remote health-care centers and slum areas. All this is done with the objective of rebuilding health structures to acceptable levels.

Oxfam International is a confederation of twelve organizations working together with over 3,000 partners in more than a hundred countries to find lasting solutions to poverty, suffering, and injustice. Its Web site explains:

> Oxfam International seeks increased worldwide public understanding that economic and social justice are crucial to sustainable development. We strive to be a global campaigning force promoting the awareness and motivation that comes with global citizenship whilst seeking to shift public opinion in order to make equity the same priority as economic growth. . . . We work with poor people. . . . We influence powerful people. . . . We join hands with all people.

World Vision International is a Christian relief and development organization providing emergency relief, education, health care, and economic development as it promotes justice.

Danny Kaye (shown here with Bing Crosby) actively supported many good causes, including the March of Dimes' fight against polio, as well as UN relief efforts.

Established in 1950 to care for orphans in Asia, World Vision today is working on six continents. In 2004, World Vision offered material, emotional, social, and spiritual support to 100 million people in ninety-six countries.

Goodwill Ambassadors

Among the best-known supporters of the United Nations are the several dozen actors, athletes, and other celebrities who serve as official Goodwill Ambassadors. On their own time, these celebrities travel the world representing the United Nations and spreading word about its work. The first Goodwill Ambassador was Danny Kaye in 1954.

UNICEF works with the world's children.

UNICEF

In the past, many Afghan children died from measles, that nation's number one killer disease. In 2002, however, that changed. Throughout the nation, loudspeakers at the mosques proclaimed, "Free measles vaccines today! Come to the mosque with your children now!" Local officials in Afghanistan teamed up with UNICEF, the United Nations Children's Fund, to immunize most Afghan children between the ages of six months and twelve years.

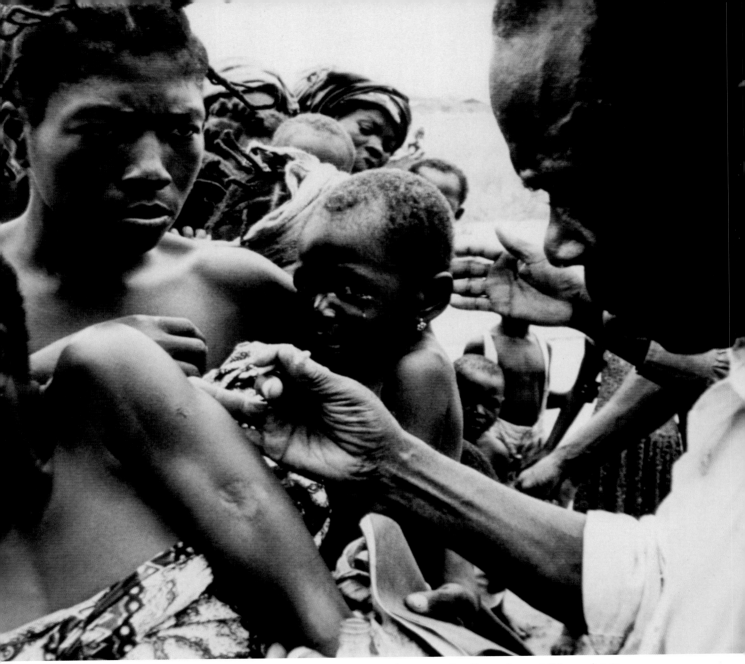

Mothers and children in the Congo receive vaccinations from UN workers.

Vaccinations are just a tiny part of the work of UNICEF: the organization helps children in 158 countries and territories providing health care and nutrition, safe water and sanitation, basic education and protection of mothers and infants. The official mission of UNICEF is "to promote the survival, protection, and development of all children worldwide." Two of its goals are "Health for All" and "Water and Sanitation for All."

History

UNICEF began as a response to the suffering of children caused by the Second World War. About fifty million people died in World War II, and the newly formed United Nations recognized that many children in Europe were in need. Children lacked food, medicine, and clothing; some children, especially babies, were dying of disease and starvation. In response to this crisis, the United Nations created a special agency for children. At first, it was called the International Children's Emergency Fund (ICEF). ICEF provided dried milk and vaccinations to the children affected by the war. In 1953, ICEF became a permanent part of the United Nations and changed its name to UNICEF.

The Declaration of the Rights of the Child

An important UN document that states the organization's commitment to human rights for children is the Declaration of the Rights of the Child. This includes the following principles:

Declaration of the Rights of the Child
Whereas mankind owes to the child the best it has to give, *Now therefore, The General Assembly Proclaims* this Declaration of the Rights of the Child. . . .
Principle 1
The child shall enjoy all the rights set forth in this Declaration. Every child, without any exception whatsoever, shall be entitled to these rights, without distinction or discrimination on account of race, colour, sex, language, religion, political or other opinion, national or social origin. . . .
Principle 2
The child shall enjoy special protection, and shall be given opportunities . . . to develop physically, mentally, morally, spiritually and socially. . . .

Principle 3

The child shall be entitled from his birth to a name and a nationality.

Principle 4

The child shall enjoy the benefits of social security. He shall be entitled to grow and develop in health. . . . The child shall have the right to adequate nutrition, housing, recreation and medical services.

Principle 5

The child who is physically, mentally or socially handicapped shall be given the special treatment, education and care required by his particular condition.

Principle 6

The child, for the full and harmonious development of his personality, needs love and understanding. He shall, wherever possible, grow up in the care and under the responsibility of his parents. . . .

Children around the world deserve love and understanding.

Children are entitled to grow up healthy, with adequate nutrition and medical services.

Children need opportunities for education and recreation.

Principle 7
The child is entitled to receive education. . . . The child shall have full opportunity for play and recreation. . . .
Principle 8
The child shall in all circumstances be among the first to receive protection and relief.
Principle 9
The child shall be protected against all forms of neglect, cruelty and exploitation. He shall not be the subject of traffic, in any form.
Principle 10
The child shall be protected from practices that may foster racial, religious and any other form of discrimination.

Funding for UNICEF

It is costly to fund UNICEF's efforts to aid children throughout the world. Most UNICEF funding comes from the governments of the UN's member nations, and individual and group donations from around the world also help out. In the United States, volunteers and workers with the U.S. Fund for UNICEF work to help reach funding goals for the organization. They visit schools and teach about the programs of UNICEF. They also raise money by selling UNICEF greeting cards.

School in a Box

Earthquakes, fires, and hurricanes can wipe out schools—but UNICEF attempts to bring learning to children even in the worst situations. Since 1990, UNICEF has been supplying "schools in a box." One box can hold everything needed to school eighty children. These boxes, packed at UNICEF's Copenhagen warehouse, are also called "edukits." The kit contains a paint and brush to turn the box lid into a blackboard: it also holds pens, a clock, books, chairs, and posters with letters, numbers, and multiplication tables. For students, the box has crayons, pencils, erasers, a pencil sharpener, rulers, and scissors. An edukit may not contain a school like yours, but it can hold everything necessary to provide children with a basic education in an emergency. In 2001, nineteen thousand edukits reached children in areas where natural disasters had removed their schools.

Humanitarian Relief Operations: Lending a Helping Hand

UNICEF allows American children to reach out and touch the lives of children living on the opposite side of the world.

One way children get involved in fund-raising for UNICEF is the "Trick or Treat for UNICEF" program. This program first began on Halloween of 1950 when some children in Philadelphia carried decorated milk cartons from house to house to collect coins for poor children overseas: that year they raised just $17. Since then, however, trick-or-treaters for UNICEF have raised more than $188 million for the organization.

Organization

The executive board, made up of thirty-six members who serve three-year terms, runs UNICEF. Seats on the board are divided up by regions of the world: Africa gets eight members, Asia seven, Eastern Europe four, Latin America together with the Caribbean five, and Western Europe, Japan and the United States twelve.

The directives of the executive board are put into action by the secretariat, run by the executive director. The first executive director was Maurice Pate, who served from 1946 to 1965.

Halloween trick-or-treaters can help raise money for UNICEF.

Children in Tanzania can benefit from UNICEF's help.

Immunizations and Childhood Diseases

After World War II, **_tuberculosis (TB)_** threatened the survivors of war, especially children. TB was called "the white plague" because the disease gave victims a very pale color. In 1947, the Red Cross began to vaccinate children in Europe, and they asked UNICEF to assist. It was the largest vaccination program ever attempted, and it was the start of UNICEF's work to improve the health of children around the globe.

Over the past five decades, UNICEF has provided vaccinations for children around the globe, making some parts of the world free from certain diseases. The Caribbean and Latin America have not seen a new case of **_polio_** in more than a decade, and China was likewise declared polio-free in 2001. UNICEF today is working in Angola and the Democratic Republic of the Congo to rid those countries of polio as well.

Nutrition and Hunger

No one likes to think about hungry children. When we see commercials for relief agencies that show us rail-thin boys and girls, we may turn the channel—or maybe we decide to give money to the organization. At any rate, we go about our daily business and soon forget that somewhere people are hungry. Unfortunately, in many parts of the world, people cannot "turn the channel" on their hunger, nor can they ever forget it. And yet freedom from hunger is one of the most basic of human rights.

Since UNICEF began, one of its priorities has been feeding children. In war-ravaged Europe in the 1940s and in Africa in the 1950s, malnutrition was common. As a response, UNICEF provided dairy products, of which the United States had a surplus at the time.

Though its early efforts were effective, UNICEF has not always done a perfect job combating malnutrition. In the 1950s and '60s, UNICEF relied on the results of a study claiming that global malnutrition was mostly the result of too little protein. Therefore, the United Nations spent time and money at food production plants in Algeria, Chile, Guatemala, and Indonesia grinding soybeans, peanuts, fish, and oils into special high-protein mixtures. Unfortunately, the resulting products were expensive and tasted horrible. Then, after all that work, experts found the earlier study was wrong: lack of protein wasn't the main problem in worldwide malnutrition. The real problem was simply lack of adequate amounts of locally produced food in much of the world, so UNICEF began working harder to improve local food production.

In Somalia, half a million people were hungry in 2005. Drought and war have kept food scarce.

Humanitarian Relief Operations: Lending a Helping Hand

UNICEF distributes high-protein biscuits and specially treated milk for Somali children. They did the same for Iraqi children in 2003. Fourteen million people in the Horn of Africa spent much of 2002 lacking enough food and water, although only a year before, UNICEF and nongovernmental organizations (NGOs) had worked hard to prevent famine in that area. UNICEF responded to the emergency by providing mass quantities of a high-nutrition mixture called Unimix, which contains corn, beans, oil, and sugar. Although UNICEF and other organizations work tirelessly to raise awareness and provide food, thousands of children still starve to death around the world each year.

AIDS

Since 1981, more than 25 million people have died from AIDS. The disease may be passed on from an infected mother to her unborn child; it is also spread through sexual contact or by using an infected needle. It first enters the bloodstream as a virus called HIV, and many people live a long time with HIV without coming down with the often-deadly AIDS.

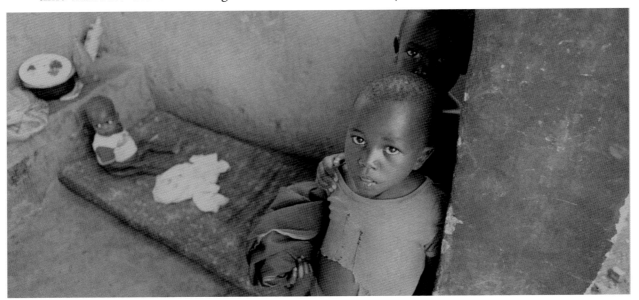

Hunger and poverty are still major problems for children around the globe.

HIV+
vaccine

A vaccination for HIV/AIDS is still just a hope. In the meantime, some 40.3 million people around the world lived with this disease in 2005.

Education is one of the best ways to combat AIDS.

In 2005, some 40.3 million people around the world lived with HIV/AIDS. Almost 5 million people contracted the disease in the same year, and more than 3 million died from the disease. Young people (15–24 years old) account for half of all new HIV infections worldwide, and more than 6,000 become infected with HIV every day. Africa has 12 million AIDS orphans.

UNICEF educates young people in epidemic-stricken nations about the ways HIV/AIDS spreads. One way UNICEF does this is through peer discussion groups, where young people in a nation can help others to protect themselves from contacting the disease. Some UNICEF AIDS programs provide testing so people can know if they are infected, and provide condoms to help protect sexually active teens.

Providing Safe Water

You probably don't think much about clean water. We assume we can turn on the tap at any time and get water to drink or wash things in. However, for millions of people in developing countries, lack of clean water is an everyday struggle. Cholera and other diseases and conditions like diarrhea result from dirty water and poor sanitation. Cholera is a disease that attacks stomachs and intestines, and it can be deadly. For well-fed and healthy people, diarrhea is just an inconvenience. However, for people already weakened and malnourished, diarrhea can also kill. Poor sanitation happens when communities lack ways to remove human and animal waste and keep water supplies clean.

Around the world, more than 1 billion people lack safe drinking water. This is despite the fact that in most parts of the world there is clean, unpolluted ***groundwater*** available beneath communities. Poor villages may lack access to clean groundwater because they don't have an affordable means to bring the water to the surface. UNICEF programs provide hand pumps that are inexpensive to install and maintain, and that are environmentally friendly. A hand pump can be positioned right over a village well; it does not require electricity or gas to operate. In twenty years, more than one billion people in over forty nations have gained access to clean, safe water by means of hand pumps.

Sometimes, disasters cause a shortage of water. An earthquake in 2001, for example, damaged water and sanitation systems in Gujarat, India. In response, UNICEF set up more than 3,400 tanks to hold water temporarily. The same year, earthquakes in El Salvador left 700,000 people without safe water as the earthquakes destroyed water and sanitation systems. UNICEF drove in trucks full of water and provided chlorine to treat wells and water systems. In 2002, after a cease-fire from war in Angola, millions of people were at risk from lack of clean water. Once again, UNICEF stepped in to help; in this case they provided pipes, pumps, cement, and advice so that communities could set up clean drinking and sanitation systems.

Education

In the 1970s, UNICEF began thinking about ways to help provide education for poor children in developing nations. Children in rural areas often do not have the chance to go to school that urban children have; they often have to help their family or community by earning a living. In some countries, literacy (the ability to read and write) was actually dropping. UNICEF knew something had to be done. Today, UNICEF allocates 20 percent of its program budget to education, especially the education of girls.

UNICEF looked at a successful experiment in Colombia's rural schools. In these areas, teachers and books were in short supply, so the *Escuela Nueva* (New School) program grouped teachers and students together as needed to make supplies stretch; teachers stressed the most practical

Healthy livestock depend on clean water sources.

Clean water is an essential human right.

One-third of all households in developing nations are headed by women.

skills needed for students to find work in their communities. Between 1985 and 1989, UNICEF worked with the Colombian government to expand schools in rural areas; as a result, they added ten thousand new schools in half a decade, and this enabled Colombia's children to gain reading and writing skills rapidly.

In some nations, constant warfare and threatened violence prevent children from going to school. In 2002, in Angola, a million children were unable to attend schools. Warfare had destroyed school buildings and supplies, and caused a lack of trained teachers. UNICEF organized training programs that trained 1,500 teachers and assistants for children in refugee camps. They also helped start mini-school programs to provide basic reading and writing skills for twenty thousand refugee children, and donated learning materials to 120,000 children in the area.

Women's Rights

Throughout its history, UNICEF has been concerned for the rights and health of mothers and babies. Issues of concern have been making childbirth safer and the right to breastfeed infants. In the past few decades, UNICEF workers realized they needed to assist women in areas other than motherhood. In the developing world, women work as educators, mothers, farmers, workers, and community leaders; one-third of households in developing nations are headed by women, and yet women still face unequal treatment and abuse.

One area of special concern to UNICEF is female genital abuse (FMG). In certain cultures, it is customary to cut girls' genitals. FMG has no medical benefit, and it robs girls of their dignity and makes them ashamed to be female: in short, it is abusive. UNICEF workers, along with many people around the world, are actively opposing this practice.

Child Refugees

From its founding, UNICEF has worked to help children in emergencies. This is still an important goal for the organization today. Children who are refugees or internally displaced persons face many challenges. They often crowd together in camps, and such crowding causes danger of sickness and shortages of food or water. UNICEF sends kits of special supplies to these camps.

When UNICEF hears of a refugee situation or other disaster, its warehouse staff in Copenhagen, Denmark, sets quickly to work preparing emergency response kits: it has twenty-nine different kits for different situations. These are usually prepared within twenty-four hours and shipped out to their destinations. In 2001, UNICEF shipped more than seventy-five thousand emergency response kits to eighty-four different countries.

Children live difficult lives in refugee camps.

Life in refugee camps is not easy. Children live in crowded tents with other family members. They have to use bathrooms used by many other people. They have to wait in line for everything they need to live: water, food, firewood, or medical care. In some cases, people are refugees for only a few weeks, but in other cases, they have to wait until a war is over or a political situation is settled. UNICEF works to make these difficult situations as livable as possible.

However, UNICEF is not the only part of the United Nations concerned with human rights. The protection of human rights is central to the UN's entire identity.

The UN often acts as the Earth's first line of defense against crises of many kinds.

Chapter 4

The United Nations in Action

When an earthquake struck the city of Kobe, Japan, on January 17, 1995, more than a million volunteers came from all over Japan to help survivors rebuild. The same was true in Thailand, Sri Lanka, and Indonesia after the 2004 tsunami; thousands of local citizens and foreign tourists gave days and weeks to help the official relief effort. According to Ramanathan Balakrishnan of UN Volunteers, an agency that mobilizes international volunteers to support sustainable development, "Volunteers form the first line of response in the aftermath of any disaster."

The UN goes to work whenever disaster hits, as it did during the tsunami of 2004.

The first twenty-four hours after a disaster strikes are the most critical, as it is still possible then for rescuers to save lives. Immediately after a disaster, volunteers work to evacuate flood or fire victims, search for people trapped in rubble, or remove bodies. Volunteers often provide for victims' most urgent needs such as first aid, medicine, and food, often from their own meager resources. "In Sri Lanka alone," said Balakrishnan, "around 300,000 volunteers contributed to the immediate relief efforts. The valuation of this effort could well exceed millions of dollars."

Some NGOs have quick-response systems that enable them to mobilize and transport disaster response resources over huge distances in a very short time. MSF uses its "Kit 10,000," a ready-made unit that contains necessary equipment to provide emergency medical relief to 10,000 disaster victims. The kit can be shipped in cargo planes within hours of a disaster. The United Nations has a team of disaster-management professionals called the Disaster Assessment and Coordination Unit (UNDAC), which is always on stand-by and can be sent to disaster sites within twenty-four hours.

It is difficult to develop networks of volunteer workers. Some religious groups have large volunteer networks that are available for certain regions, but of all volunteer-based organizations, the

A hurricane kit provides basic necessities.

After the Hurricane

Jaime Velasquez Bautista of Guatemala lost his wife on October 5, 2005, while trying to save his two oldest daughters from mudslides that occurred during Hurricane Stan. Two months later, with five children to feed and a broken arm, he was out of work and hungry.

Days before Christmas in 2005, the WFP was continuing nonstop food distributions to more than 300,000 Guatemalans devastated by Hurricane Stan. "WFP wants to make sure that every single child, woman and man affected by Stan is not left without food during the coming holidays," said WFP Guatemala Emergency Coordinator Helmut Rauch. "We've heard and seen enough distress in the field, and we've heard too many heartbreaking stories; it's now time for people to concentrate on rebuilding their lives. WFP food will enable them to do just that." Thanks to the WFP, Jaime Velasquez Bautista and his children didn't spend Christmas 2005 with empty stomachs.

IFRC (International Federation of the Red Cross) is the largest and best organized. Volunteers are at its very heart, and have been since it began in 1863. The IFRC claims 97 million members in the Red Cross/Red Crescent Movement worldwide, an estimated 20 million of whom are volunteers.

The United Nations and the Tsunami

The United Nations responded quickly and on a massive scale to the devastation of the 2004 tsunami, with efforts ranging from water storage tanks in India to safe-delivery kits for pregnant women in the Maldives to fishery experts in Indonesia. UN workers ran five parallel operations tending to the needs of nearly a dozen countries struck by the catastrophe. In India, where contaminated water threatened to spread deadly diseases in the tsunami's aftermath, UNICEF delivered nearly 2,500 500-liter water storage tanks to relief camps and distributed 3 million water purification chlorine tablets. In Indonesia, UNHCR airlifted 400 tons of shelter and other emergency supplies. In the Maldives, the UN Population Fund (UNFPA) provided safe-delivery kits for 4,000 expectant mothers, while UNICEF provided food and shelter. In Sri Lanka, UNICEF provided 10,000 bed sheets, towels, drinking water bottles, cooking utensils sets, and mats to assist the displaced and stranded. In Thailand, UNFPA deployed mobile clinics, and the UNDP sent 1,000 body bags to the devastated holiday resort of Phuket.

Hurricane Katrina left disaster in its wake.

Secretary-General Kofi Annan

The Thailand resort city of Phuket was devastated by the tsunami.

On April 13, 2005, Secretary-General Kofi Annan made the following remarks at a news conference:

It's now nearly 100 days since the United Nations was asked to take the lead in coordinating relief efforts for the victims of the tsunami. It was a massive and daunting challenge. . . . Even now, we continue to see pictures and hear stories of the terrible devastation caused by this unprecedented disaster. But the effects of the tragedy have largely faded—as we knew they would—from the front pages and from our nightly news. So it's vitally important that we have someone capable of sustaining international interest in the fate of the survivors and their communities—and someone with vision and commitment to ensure that, this time, the international community really does follow through and support the people and the transition from immediate relief to longer-term recovery and reconstruction. Too often, in the aftermath of previous natural disasters, that has not been the case.

To make sure that the needs of communities hit by the tsunami remain in the news, Kofi Annan appointed former U.S. president Bill Clinton to serve as UN Special Envoy to Tsunami-affected Countries.

A year after the tsunami, UN Emergency Relief Coordinator, Jan Egeland, noted that the tsunami "was only the beginning in what was to become the Year of Disasters," and urged world's citizens to provide humanitarian agencies with the funds they need before tragedy strikes.

Imagine if your local fire department had to beg the mayor for money to turn on the water hoses every time a fire broke out. Now imagine numerous fires occurring simultaneously all over the globe, but no money on hand to turn on the hoses. That's the situation faced by aid workers whenever a major crisis erupts.

Disaster Prevention and Preparedness

According to the Emergency Events Database (EMDAT), a project that gathers statistics related to disasters, natural disasters are more frequent and more deadly now than they have been in the past. One reason for this is climate change; this has recently caused a greater number of ocean and weather related disasters. Hurricanes, tidal waves, and earthquakes have grown more common than ever before, and this trend is expected to continue.

Feng Min Kan directs the International Strategy for Disaster Reduction (ISDR) for Africa, a UN agency that works with African governments on disaster risk reduction (DRR). Kan says:

The 1970s witnessed a growing sense that disaster risks can actually be reduced. In the 1980s, the damage caused by natural disasters increased dramatically. This is what led to the adoption of the International Decade for Natural Disaster Reduction during the 1990s.

In 1989, the General Assembly proclaimed the coming decade "the International Decade for

Former president Bill Clinton was appointed as the UN's special envoy to tsunami-affected nations.

Natural Disaster Reduction" (IDNDR). The United Nations sought to provide a global disaster-reduction "roadmap." The IDNDR aimed to increase the disaster response ability of countries, especially by emphasizing early-warning systems. In 2001, The ISDR secretariat was established in Geneva, Switzerland, to work on DRR strategies and policies.

A World Disaster Reduction Conference was held in January 2005 in Kobe, Japan. As one participant reported, "There was a time when we did not know where disasters would strike. But today we know which countries are most disaster prone. Flooding in Bangladesh and drought in Ethiopia are hardly a surprise." Participants noted disappointment, however, that in many nations, DRR information and proposals failed to make it from suggestion to action. Three weeks before the Kobe meeting, the tsunami struck: a horrific reminder that disaster reduction needs to be taken much more seriously throughout the world. UN under-secretary general Jan Egeland said to the conference, "The best way to honour the dead is to protect the living. Good intentions must be turned into concrete action."

Time Line

October 24, 1945   United Nations Day, approval of the UN Charter.

1945   United Nations Development Programme (UNDP) is founded.

1946   The International Children's Emergency Fund (ICEF) is created.

1947   Tuberculosis vaccinations are given around the world.

1949   UNRWA, the United Nations Relief and Works Agency, is established.

1950   Office of the United Nations High Commissioner for Refugees (UNHCR) begins.

1953   ICEF becomes UNICEF (United Nations Children's Fund).

1954   Danny Kaye becomes the United Nations' first Goodwill Ambassador.

1959   Declaration of the Rights of the Child is formulated.

1965   UNICEF receives Nobel Peace Prize for "promotion of brotherhood between nations."

1979   UNICEF declares the International Year of the Child.

1980   The long battle against smallpox is spearheaded by the World Health Organization.

1981   World AIDS/HIV epidemic begins.

1990   Beginning of the International Decade for Natural Disaster Reduction (IDNDR). UNICEF begins "School in a Box."

1994   José Ayala Lasso is first UN High Commissioner for Human Rights.

1996   Iraq oil-for-food program begins.

2000	Millennium Assembly sets goals for world health and social development.
2001	Aid workers are killed in Afghanistan.
2004	Tsunami disaster in Asia prompts massive relief effort.
2005	Bill Clinton is named Special Envoy to tsunami-affected countries.

Glossary

asylum: A place of safety.

controversy: Something that causes disagreement.

discrimination: Unfair treatment of one person or group, usually because of prejudice about race, ethnic group, age group, religion, or gender.

disenfranchised: Deprived someone of a privilege, immunity, or legal right.

dispensaries: Places where medical supplies are stored and distributed to patients by a pharmacist.

displaced persons: People who are forced to leave their own homes or countries, especially because of war or political oppression.

epidemic: An outbreak of a disease that spreads more quickly and more extensively among a group of people than would normally be expected.

exiles: Those who are forced to leave their homes.

groundwater: Water within the earth that supplies wells and springs.

guerrillas: Fighters who engage in irregular warfare that usually involves sabotage and harassment.

humanitarian: Concerned with the well-being of others.

intelligence service: An agency that obtains information about an enemy or possible enemy.

internally displaced: Forced to leave homes or residences, in particular as a result of or in order to avoid the effects of armed conflict, situations of generalized violence, violations of human rights, or natural or human-made disasters, without crossing an internationally recognized country border.

latrines: Communal toilets on a military base.

nongovernmental organizations (NGOs): Independent organizations that are not part of the government and were not founded by the state.

paramilitaries: Fighting units that are modeled on, but not part of, the military.

polio: Poliomyelitis; a severe infectious disease that inflames the brain stem and spinal cord, sometimes leading to paralysis and muscular wasting.

sanitation: Procedures related to the collection and disposal of sewage and garbage.

tuberculosis (TB): An infectious disease that causes small rounded swellings to form on mucous membranes and affects the lungs.

Further Reading

Brenner, Barbara. *The United Nations 50th Anniversary Book.* New York: Simon & Schuster, 1995.

Fasulo, Linda. *An Insider's Guide to the UN.* New Haven, Conn.: Yale University Press, 2004.

Grahame, Deborah A. *UNICEF.* Milwaukee, Wis.: World Almanac Library, 2004.

Jacobs, William Jay. *Search for Peace: The Story of the United Nations.* New York: Charles Scribner's Sons, 2004.

Woog, Adam. *The United Nations.* San Diego, Calif.: Lucent, 2004.

For More Information

Médecins Sans Frontiers
www.msf.org

Oxfam International
www.oxfam.org/en

The UN in Brief
www.un.org/Overview/brief.html

United Nations Development Programme
www.undp.org

UNICEF Somalia
www.unicef.org/somalia/index.html

UNRWA
www.un.org/unrwa

The World Food Program
www.wfp.org/english

World Vision International
www.wvi.org/wvi/home.htm

Publisher's note:
The Web sites listed on this page were active at the time of publication. The publisher is not responsible for Web sites that have changed their addresses or discontinued operation since the date of publication. The publisher will review and update the Web-site list upon each reprint.

Reports and Projects

Written Reports

• Write a report about a recent international disaster or crisis.
• Research news sites on the Internet and report on what the United Nations is doing in humanitarian assistance this week.
• Write to offices of the United Nations regarding a current disaster or crisis; ask what it is doing to respond.
• Write a report on what areas of the world are most likely to face major disasters in the near future and how they can prepare for that.

Oral Reports/Drama/Media/Debate
• Imagine you are a citizen of tsunami-hit Sri Lanka, Indonesia, or earthquake-hit Pakistan, and tell how the UN response to the disaster helped your life.
• Form teams and debate the topic: "The UN does (or does not) work well to prepare for and respond to disasters."
• Do a multimedia presentation (PowerPoint, collage, or CD/DVD with accompanying oral report) about the UN response to a disaster or crisis.
• Work in a group. Pretend you each represent a different continent. Together, come up with a plan for needed humanitarian assistance in the twenty-first century.

Bibliography

Assadourian, Erik, Hilary French, and Michael Renner. *State of the World 2005: A Worldwatch Institute Report on Progress Toward a Sustainable Society.* New York: Worldwatch Institute, 2005.

The Heritage Foundation: Oil-for-Food Audits.
    http://www.heritage.org/Research/InternationalOrganizations/wm638.cfm. (accessed January 12, 2005)

IRIN.news. http://www.irinnews.org.

Office of Iraq Programme: Oil-for-food. http://www.un.org/Depts/oip/index.html.
Relief Web. http://www.reliefweb.int/rw/dbc.nsf/doc100?OpenForm.

Index

85

Picture Credits

Benjamin Stewart: pp. 71, 73
Corbis: pp. 52, 54
Corel: pp. 13, 15, 16, 18, 20, 22, 25, 26, 27, 29, 31, 40, 44, 46, 48, 49, 50, 58, 60, 61, 62
Fight to the Finish: Stories of Polio: p. 42
iStockphotos: pp. 57, 66, 68, 69
    Dor Jordan: pp. 32, 33
    Grace Tan: p. 8
    Justin Long: p. 10
    Klass Lingbeekvan Kranen: pp. 36, 39
    Luis Alvarez: p. 34
Photos.com: pp. 14, 35, 53
PhotoSpin: pp. 56, 64
United Nations: p. 72
U.S. Library of Congress: p. 75

To the best knowledge of the publisher, all other images are in the public domain. If any image has been inadvertently uncredited, please notify Harding House Publishing Service, Vestal, New York 13850, so that rectification can be made for future printings.

Biographies

Author

Roger Smith is a writer who previously spent a decade teaching junior high school in a multiethnic setting. He has traveled to the Middle East and Central America and has participated in organizations committed to world peace and human rights issues.

Series Consultant

Bruce Russett is Dean Acheson Professor of Political Science at Yale University and editor of the *Journal of Conflict Resolution*. He has taught or researched at Columbia, Harvard, M.I.T., Michigan, and North Carolina in the United States, and educational institutions in Belgium, Britain, Israel, Japan, and the Netherlands. He has been president of the International Studies Association and the Peace Science Society, holds an honorary doctorate from Uppsala University in Sweden. He was principal adviser to the U.S. Catholic Bishops for their pastoral letter on nuclear deterrence in 1985, and co-directed the staff for the 1995 Ford Foundation Report, *The United Nations in Its Second Half Century*. He has served as editor of the *Journal of Conflict Resolution* since 1973. The twenty-five books he has published include *The Once and Future Security Council* (1997), *Triangulating Peace: Democracy, Interdependence, and International Organizations* (2001), *World Politics: The Menu for Choice* (8th edition 2006), and *Purpose and Policy in the Global Community* (2006).